ETIQUETTE & STYLE BY DUPREE

WHOSE FORK IS IT Anyway?

DINING ETIQUETTE GUIDE FOR TEENS

TONI DUPREE

Whose Fork is it Anyway?
Copyright © 2015 by Toni Dupree
Cover & Interior Design:
TamikaInk.com
Photo by: Emile C. Browne
ISBN-13: 978-1515311119
LCCN: 2015914810

This book was printed in the United States.

DEDICATION

This book is dedicated to my mother, Jydelle M. Taylor. I attended charm and etiquette classes beginning at the age of 5. My mother, who I affectionately called "JT," always told me there is wealth in being well-behaved. My mother instilled values in me by showing me my worth by teaching me how to invest in others. This great lesson has helped me build a brand based on a strong foundation of leadership, trust, decency and grace. I am blessed to enrich a community of people with knowledge by simply pouring quality and respect into our society.

I am so grateful to my mother for showing me my purpose so early in life. She would always tell me, "You are unique, built for the hard stuff and destined to do great things." This book is proof that she was right!

With All My Love,
Toni Dupree

ACKNOWLEDGEMENTS

There are so many people who have supported me on this profound journey of etiquette. My girlfriends who have inspired me to stay grounded and balanced I am truly grateful for your unconditional love.

To my colleagues and friends who keep me busy and on task, I appreciate your commitment and respect for my vision. To everyone who worked on this project, thank you so much for your creativity and ingenuity in making it a reality.

To my mentor, the brilliant Lew Bayer I appreciate you for investing in my dream and supporting my purpose for my life and being a great friend. Canada certainly has a real jewel in its midst!

To my publisher, Tamika Hall of TamikaInk.com, thank you for your patience and most of all I appreciate you for helping me bring my passion to life.

Mr. Lloyd Sowell, you are amazing! Thank you so much for sharing your talent, for ministering to me, and for your support.

Ms.Merry Payne you were a lovely angel, thank you you for housing me during the flood and allowing me to use your computer to get my book finished.

FOREWORD

As we look around us, we see so many examples of uncivil, rude behavior, and poor habits amongst the adults in society. We wonder what has happened? Where did manners fall by the wayside? In years past, people seemed to be on their best behaviors when in the public eye. I think it goes back to our grandparents and their generation. I remember my grandmother and great-aunts taking special care to correct me if I put my elbows on the tables as I ate, or chewed my meal with my mouth open, less I embarrass them on a public outing and appear to 'be raised by wolves', one of the frequent descriptions I heard often. I haven't forgotten those lessons and I've passed them down to my children.

But everyone doesn't have a grandmother or great-aunt to help them navigate the seemingly complex rules of etiquette these days. That's where this book comes in. Toni Dupree has brought a common-sense and modern approach to "old-school" table etiquette, bringing its importance to the 21st century, making it fun, cool and even hip to know "Whose Fork is it Anyway"!

Roslyn A. Grizzard RDMS, RVT CHTS-PW

The Story

Toni woke up very early this particular morning because she had an idea for dinner with her girlfriends Michelle, Tootsie and Tracy. Toni really needed her mother Jydelle's help. She tried to wait until her mother woke up, but she just couldn't because her idea was just too exciting! Toni went into her mother's bedroom at 5:00am and began to wake her.

Toni pushed her mom and yelled "Mommy, Mommy...please, oh please, wake up! It's very important!" Jydelle woke up slightly irritated, thinking something serious was happening, like the house may have been on fire.

"What is it, what is it, Toni?"

"Mommy, I want to have a dinner party with Michelle, Tootsie and Tracy. We have to get started soon! Toni's mom asked,

"When do you want to have this dinner party?"

Toni thought about it and said with hesitation, "This weekend, How about this weekend, Mommy?"

"I think we can swing that, but sweetie you haven't planned or hosted a dinner party before. There are some things we have to go over to ensure you and your friends will have a quality dining experience."

"Like what, Mommy? What is it that we need to know? We know how to feed ourselves and eat. I'm willing to help you prepare the meal."

"Well, thank you, my dear. That is very sweet of you and I am so glad that you are willing to help prepare the meal because that's a big part of a dinner party."

"I figured that Mommy."

Later that day, Toni and her mom started working on the dinner party plans.

Toni's mom said, "Now, Toni, we need to go over some important details which will guarantee a great dining experience for you and your friends."

"What are those details, Mommy?"

"Well those details are understanding the American Style of dining, setting the table, how to cut our food, proper eating techniques, appropriate dining posture, the best dining conversation topics, finish position for utensils, napkin placement."

"Wow! That's a lot, Mommy! I just wanted to have dinner with my friends."

"I understand, Toni. But, it's very important to know the proper way to dine because this will not be the only dining experience you and your friends will have in your lifetime. I am very proud of you for wanting to create this dining experience with your friends."

"Thank you, Mommy. I just wanted us to do something different. It just came to me when I woke up this morning. We go out to eat all of the time, but this will be better because it's customized just for us."

Jydelle was so proud of her daughter for taking the initiative to plan this dinner party for her friends that she wanted to prepare a very special meal fit for the occasion. She asked Toni what they wanted for dinner because she would have to go to the grocery store.

Toni said, "What about Roast, Au Gratin Potatoes, vegetables, Mac and Cheese, and Butter Pecan Ice Cream for dessert?"

Jydelle replied, "Au Gratin Potatoes or Mac and Cheese, not both, Sweetie."

"Aww, man...it's my dinner party!"

"I understand, but I'm your mother, and I say one or the other."

"Ok...Au Gratin Potatoes then."

"Good job choosing your menu, Honey."

"Thank you, Mommy."

"Before we go to the grocery store, call Michelle, Tootsie and Tracy and ask them to come over earlier while dinner is cooking for a short dining etiquette lesson."

"Ok, Mommy. I will go call them right now. This is going to be so much fun! Thank you!"

"You are very welcome, my love."

Later that afternoon when Jydelle and Toni were back from the grocery store the girls came over to their house. While Jydelle was getting dinner started, she called the girls in to begin the lesson. Toni used a casual dinner setting for the table and girl's hands were resting on their laps while listening to Jydelle give instructions.

The
Lesson

AMERICAN STYLE OF DINING

- The fork is held in the left hand and the knife is held in the right hand when cutting food.
- Make a gliding motion, positing the knife behind the fork.
- Bring the food to your mouth with the fork prongs facing upward.

SIGNALING TO PAUSE OR WHEN FINSIHED WITH YOUR MEAL

RESTING POSITION　　　　　　**FINISHED POSITION**

- If you need to pause during dinner, place your utensil in the resting position. The knife on the right side of the plate with blade facing in, and fork facing the left side with the prongs upward. The resting position is very important for a couple of reasons. First, it signals to your waiter that you aren't finished with your meal. Second, it prevents your knife and fork from sliding off of your plate.
- When you are finished with your meal, pretend your plate is a clock, and plate both handles of your utensils in the "four o'clock." (See picture above for an example)

THE FORMAL SETTING

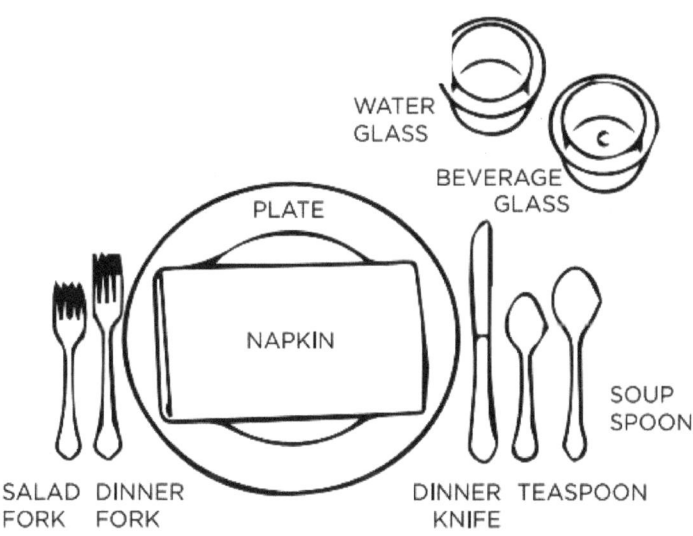

WATER GLASS

BEVERAGE GLASS

PLATE

NAPKIN

SOUP SPOON

SALAD FORK   DINNER FORK

DINNER KNIFE   TEASPOON

THE CASUAL SETTING

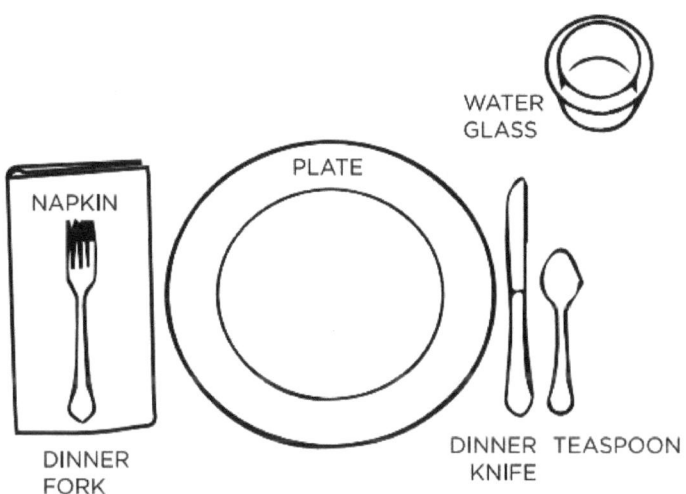

WATER GLASS

PLATE

NAPKIN

DINNER FORK

DINNER KNIFE   TEASPOON

APPROPRIATE DINING POSTURE

Good posture while dining helps boost your confidence, as well as aid in your digestion.

Helpful Hints:
- Scoot close to the table, leaving little room between your stomach and the table.
- Make sure to lightly press your back against the chair to prevent slouching.
- Be mindful not to cross your legs under the table. This may cause slouching and poor digestion.
- While holding a utensil with one hand, the other should rest in your lap. You can also place both hands in your lap on top of your napkin, if needed.
- Always ask someone near any objects you need to pass them to you. If you reach for them yourself you risk ruining your great dining posture, as well as being considered rude for reaching over others and invading their space.

Tips To Avoid Inappropriate posture
- Don't Slouch
- Your belly button should be three inches from the table. This will allow you to have perfect table posture.

APPROPRIATE DINNER CONVERSATION

- Conversation has to involve more than one person, otherwise it's a speech. It is always good practice to ask open ended questions in an effort to keep dinner guest engaged in a well-rounded conversation.
- Dinner conversation should be light and inviting. Topics should be appropriated thereby keeping guest comfortable and entertained during dinner.
- Make sure to go around the table to engage and connect with your guests. This offers an opportunity to network on your level as well deterring guest from using their cell phones during dinner.

Tips for successful dinner conversation

- Today, conversation at the table usually involves two or three people sitting next to one another. If you notice one of your neighbors is left with no one to talk to, include him/her in the conversation by first conducting an introduction. Tell the group something interesting about that person that will spark more enlightening conversation.
- If you have nothing in common with your neighbor, listen around for common interest. For example, conversation regarding the food, school, family, or extra- curricular activities.

CELL PHONE ETIQUETTE

DON'T

- Don't put your cell phone on the table during a meal; it sends a message of disrespect and disregard no matter who you are dining with. It is the equivalent of telling your dining guest that whomever may be texting, emailing, or calling you is more important than they are.
- **Don't Use your phone in the company of your guest.** If you must take a call excuse yourself for a moment then promptly return to your dinner guest.

NAPKIN PLACEMENT

- Casual Dining: The napkin can be placed directly on top of the dinner plate when setting the table.
- Formal Dining: the napkin always goes on the left side of the plate along with the dinner fork and salad fork. The knife goes on the right with the soup and teaspoons.
- Excusing yourself: when you excuse yourself from the table temporarily place your napkin on chair to signal that you will be returning.

The Do's & Don'ts

- **Do** let soup cool, then swallow.
- **Don't** slurp your soup.
- **Do** put one hand in your lap during dinner.
- **Don't** eat with both hands on the table.
- **Do** bring your food to you.
- **Don't** bend over to "go after" your food.

- **Do** chew bite-sized pieces of food.
- **Don't** bite off more than you can chew.
- **Do** lay your napkin across your lap while you wait to be served.
- **Don't** stuff your napkin in your shirt.

- **Do** excuse yourself to blow your nose in an effort not to disturb everyone's dining experience.
- **Don't** blow your nose at the table.
- **Do** pass the salt and pepper together, never separately.
- **Don't** sanitize your hands at the table.

DINING TIPS

- Once seated, placed the napkin across your lap.
- Always serve the lady sitting to the right of host (the person who extended the dinner invitation) first, then the other ladies in a clockwise direction, and lastly the men.
- Remember to hold the knife and fork with the handle in the palm of your hand, forefinger on top, and thumb underneath.
- If food presented is not to your liking, it is polite to make an attempt to eat small amounts or cut it up and move it around the plate to show a good faith effort.
- Dessert may be eaten with both spoon and fork.
- When a lady excuses herself from the table, it is polite for the gentlemen to stand and then sit until the lady returns. When the lady returns the gentlemen should stand again.
- Always thank the hostess (female) or host (male).

We learned so much during our dining lesson with my mother and had so much fun! She surprised us with take aways a colorful guide of dining do's and dont's also, highlighting tips for best dining techniques. Dinner was amazing, of course. Mommy is a great cook although we have had her cooking a million times. We couldn't believe how much she taught us about dining etiquette. I am so excited that everything went off without a hitch. And what's more exciting is Michelle, Tootsie, Tracy and I have decided to take turns hosting dinner parties. We also agreed to invite one or two other friends to join in on the fun. We are calling our dinner parties the "Whose Fork Is It Anyway Supper Club." My girlfriends and I had a blast eating and learning tips for dining and how to create a dining experience with my mom. We can't wait to have the first, Whose Fork Is It Anyway Supper Club dining experience!

NOTES

NOTES

NOTES

NOTES

NOTES

ABOUT THE AUTHOR

Toni Dupre was born and raised in Houston, Texas where she currently lives with her well-mannered Chihuahua mix, Luchia. Toni's mother, Jydelle Taylor, was a cosmetologist who spent her time investing in her only child's cultural and social development. Toni's upbringing groomed her for her life's true passion; building character and self-esteem through Etiquette & Style by Dupree (www.etiquettestylebydupree.com), where she offers an array of social, personal, and professional development services for individuals and organizations.

Toni graduated from Interior Arts School of Designer, and has 23 years of experience as an Interior designer. She also owns Civility Experts Houston. Toni is certified as a behavior therapist, she also holds a certification with the Center for Organizational Cultural Competence in Canada. Toni is a candidate for trainer status with International Civility Trainer's Consortium, one of only 8 Master Trainers in the world. She also teaches a class called "Civility Works" for Leisure Learning Unlimited in Houston, Texas.

Toni's other works include the columns, "Etiquette in the Most Common Places," for Empower magazine and "An Etiquette Perspective," for MVMNT Magazine, a teen magazine geared to support teen spiritual awareness. Toni has been featured in the Gospel Review magazine, 40'z Rock calendar as Ms. December 2014, and creator of the app "So Rude Houston." She volunteers for Makeover 101, Villas of Winkler and a host of other organizations.

DOWNLOAD MY FREE PHONE APP

APP INFORMATION
Download the app from the iTunes store by searching for, "So Rude Houston," or scan the QR Code found to the right when using your phone.

ONLINE COURSE
Take an online Etiquette Course through MannersTV.
Visit: http://civilityexpertsonline.com for information.